Life after loss...
Healing from the inside out

When looks can be deceiving
and the inside is damaged

Keyona Kline

Copyright @Keyona Kline 2019

ISBN: 978-0-578-62808-0

This journal is dedicated to those of us who struggle through life on a daily basis; to those who have no idea how they've made it through the day, week, month, or even years; to those who fight for peace of mind in the busiest of places. For those of us who are too busy mentally, physically, and emotionally to even think of a quiet space because life won't stop; you want nothing more than to turn the volume down, but there's no mute button. To those who walk through life and no one is aware that there is even a problem. To those of us who try to escape life in any way we possibly can.

Special thank you to Karen Jones, my step mother, for always being in my corner and helping me with anything I ask without hesitation. To my sisters that I drive crazy on a regular basis, I thank you all for being there for me to offer any type of support you can, have, and continue to do. To my husband and children, I know life with me is not always easy but I'm forever grateful for your unconditional love. Without you my life would be meaningless. I love you all so deeply and please know I do my best because I'm counting on you counting on me.

Thank you to all those who continue to encourage and support us. We appreciate your continued support!

Psychiatrist Elisabeth Kubler-Ross developed a theory that suggests that we go through five stages of grief: **denial, anger, bargaining, depression,** then **acceptance**. Grief can be experienced regardless of what the loss may be; a loss is a loss, be it a job, marriage, home or the passing of a loved one. Grief is also very personal and one person can not say when or how grief may affect another. There is no right or wrong way to grieve and per several studies, someone may experience all five stages, or they may not experience any of the five stages of the grief process. That's what makes grief so personal. There's no order in which we should grieve or a length of time we should have to determine when our grief should end.

Society has a way of making us feel as if we have to rush through life, when in actuality, we should take a step back and reevaluate our own life circumstances - without our emotions or society's interference. We need to slow ourselves and learn to take as much time as we may need. Somehow, some way, others seem to make our grief about them, disregarding our feelings or emotions to our life circumstances.

Living out loud has a new meaning because in 2019 social media is the thing to do — we all live through the photographs of others, without knowing the true story behind the picture. Maybe she's recently divorced, but traveling and smiling in every photo she posts, but deep down inside she needs the public's acceptance because she's lonely or depressed. We are so quick to want what everyone else looks like they have. We would never know a depressed widow, a divorced woman, a childless mother, or fatherless child's true feelings or life faults because that part will never be shared. It's not a secret, but that part of life no one wants to share; it doesn't look pretty. The moral of the story is, don't judge a book by its cover. Stay true to yourself and grieve your way.

"You may not control all the events that happen to you, but you can decide not to be reduced by them."

-MAYA ANGELOU

Life has a very strange way of happening to us all, be it the wrong time, wrong place, or wrong person. It forces so many questions: why me? why them? why now? and what on earth have I done to deserve this?! We all battle with something on a daily basis; some things worse than others. But whether it's good or bad, the only way to get through is to gain the knowledge needed to conquer our stress, grief, anxiety, depression, and anger.

Emotions are temporary, so we must try to read as much as we can regarding those topics to help us learn how to get through hardships when life happens. Unfortunately, we as humans sometimes experience one bad moment and immediately turn it into a bad day, month, or life. We have the tendency to automatically rule our lives a homicide once something happens to us that is out of our control, or that we never expected to happen. Of course, none of us want to go through any of the tragedies we face, but some of us have gained front row seats without spending a dime. That's life. We must learn how to get through those small situations, so that when the big ones come, we know how to handle our stress and anxiety. Positivity is a state of mind.

THE GRIEVING PROCESS

As mentioned, the Kubler-Ross model explains the five stages of grief. The first stage is **denial**. When life happens, whether it's fast or slow, under tragic circumstances or within expectancy, it's still often hard to accept. We know what is happening, but somehow we are in complete denial and incapable of handling the stress accompanied by the fear of what is to come. It is normal for all of us to fear the unknown. We want to avoid the situation as long as we possibly can, so we live completely outside of our normal lifestyles, doing things we've never done before (which, sometimes is forced upon us and completely out of our control). We avoid conversations involving the situation. We try to cope with the situation by picking up new habits like drinking, oversleeping, overspending, using drugs — anything we can do to not deal with our overwhelming emotions. Sometimes these habits are just that, habits, but other times they stick around and become addictions. In contrast to these negative emotions, feeling elated may also be an emotion we feel during this stage, depending upon the situation. The confusion and shock of it all can also be the cause of fear and anxiety, which can cause more denial and lead to anger, depression, and much more.

Anger is the next stage. We have all experienced some sort of anger in our lives, sometimes on a daily basis. When it comes to grief, anger means something different. Fear anxiety and frustration can cause an anger you've never experienced. You have several questions and, of course, "why?" is number one on the list. Why did this happen? None of us have a reason why and that alone can cause an anger that is unbearable. You are confused and want to release the anger, but you don't know how. How on earth are you supposed to keep calm at such a time? When all you can think of is anger/rage. We must have an outlet, a coach, friend, family member; some type of positive influence to get through those moments of unexplainable anger.

Bargaining is the stage that we enter when we want the answers that we will never receive. You catch yourself pleading with the higher power "God, what did I do wrong to deserve this?" " I would do anything you ask if only I could have them back". You want so badly for someone to hear your pleading and bargain with you. You expect magical moments to happen and suddenly all your questions will be answered, but we all know that will never happen. If only life was so easy.

After bargaining with no results, we experience **depression**. We want answers. We want all of our pleading to be heard, but by whom? The overwhelming emotion of completely feeling helpless causes the desire to curl up and let life go on without you. We feel empty inside; no one has answers - not even you, and it's your situation/loved one. You may have suicidal thoughts; thoughts that life would be better without you in it. That is never the answer!

The last stage is **acceptance**. Even though we want our lives to return to the "normal", unfortunately, that is not an option. We must create a new normal. You accept the fact that life as you have known it will be completely different and that no one is responsible for living the rest of your life but you, so you must make the best of it.

"Stand up straight and realize who you are, that you tower over your circumstances."

—MAYA ANGELOU

The first step to bettering yourself in any situation is to take time out for you. In many ways we get caught up in the moment and forget to take care of ourselves. Recognize and know your limits. Don't push yourself beyond a comfortable physical state and know that you are doing your best...and just because you have one bad moment, know that it won't last forever.

Know how much you can handle when it comes to special occasions. Avoid making major decisions. Try to have a plan, set boundaries. Talk with your family regarding the "firsts" of occasions after a loss (i.e., holidays, birthdays and the anniversary of the loss). Introduce something new, make it different, but memorable. Have fun and try to live in the moment and not for yesterday; for yesterday is gone to never return.

Talking has always been a good way to release pain, frustration and anxiety. Take the time to sit with someone you trust and talk weekly - daily if needed...you don't have to have a specific subject to talk about, just talk. Let whatever comes up come out. Do not hold painful feelings inside. Holding onto and not releasing the emotions can cause deeper depression. Express yourself in anyway you can...positively.

Start new habits. Taking care of your physical health is very important. Round up friends and hit the gym, go walking, or try a new activity...something you've never done before. Your diet and how much you sleep is also very important. Following a balanced diet is so tough for the working adult, and when you add stress and life to that, the diet is definitely thrown off. We eat whatever we can find. So, planning meals would help us stay on track. Try to sleep at least five to eight hours per night. Although it's very hard, we must set new goals to achieve a healthier, mind, body and soul.

Express yourself creatively. Journaling has been proven to be a great way to decrease stress and depression. It is a true outlet to let pain out on paper and without any judgement. Writing is an old tool used for expression and creativity.

Journaling has many mental health benefits. It has been proven to reduce stress, clarify thoughts, and help to release bottled up emotions. Writing can be a great tool to organize your life after any major change or tragedy. Journaling on a regular basis can help you learn new ways to get to know yourself better and resolve unresolved issues.

Remembering our loved ones is also very important... thinking of them and keeping their legacy alive is how we heal. So whatever you feel is honorable, do it yearly, or whenever you feel the need. Make every day memorable and celebrate life!

Time isn't the main thing, it's the only thing. -Miles Davis

"Stand up straight and realize who you are, that you tower over your circumstances."

-MAYA ANGELOU

MY GRIEF JOURNEY...FROM MY EYES TO YOURS

I can still hear the alarms blaring that morning as we awoke to start the day. It was 5:30am on Wednesday, October 5, 2016. I got out of bed and went directly to my boys' rooms to get them up and started for the day. After that, I headed downstairs to the kitchen to prepare breakfast. The boys filed into the kitchen to eat before we had to run out the door. My oldest son, Sean was still sleeping because he had worked the overnight shift the night before. He was the one who would usually get the younger boys to school because his dad and I worked very early shifts; but this was my off day. As I was heading back upstairs to get myself dressed, Sean was actually awake and heading down; we said good morning and I continued up. When I came back down in a rush, he was already prepared to drop them off. They were all heading for the front door, when I stated that I would take Sam, my youngest son and he could take my middle son Stanley and his friends. As we got outside, we noticed that my car had a flat tire. So, as always, Sean said "Ma, I got them" and they all headed to school. He returned about twenty five minutes later. I was in the family room preparing to do laundry. We chatted about plans for the day and decided to head out together to run some errands before Sean headed to work. Since he was working the afternoon shift at his first job, we both showered and then headed out.

We got into my car and started talking about events that had taken place over the past few days, since we hadn't really spent that much time together because of our work schedules. Mid-conversation, his cell phone rang a few times, but he didn't answer because we were conversing about his lil brother learning to drive and how he did the day before on the road with me for the first time. Once we reached our destination, the phone rang again. "Hello, what's up? I'm with dukes right now, then we're headed back to the house. I have to work at 11:30. Oh, you want me to wait for you here? Okay cool." Then he hung up. "Who was that" I asked. "Oh, that was John, he said. "Oh, what did he want?" "Nothing", he said. "He said he's off today and was bored so he was going to meet us up here." Before we could finish what we needed to do, we saw John pulling into the parking lot - driving as if he was in a rush. That was the very first day I had ever opened my mouth to speak to this young man. Sean had met John in high school; I heard his name a few times, but never really knew him. I only knew of him. I don't know what it was but my soul just never felt that he was a "FRIEND" to my son. Any time they were together, he would somehow break curfew or do something that was totally out of character.

Once John spotted my son standing outside of my car, he pulled over. They had a brief conversation before we all headed back to my home. John was driving fast and in and out of traffic. I asked, "Does he drive that way all the time?" My son looked at me and said, "Yes". I was annoyed by that time. When we reached the house, John was already parked in front waiting. Sean came in the door behind me and began upstairs to get his work uniform on. Again, I began asking questions as mothers do...Are you going to work? Why is he here? He's going to follow you to work? Why? "Ma!!!" Sean said, and we both laughed, shared a hug and an "I love you". He said that he would be home by 4:30pm. He also reminded me of the time and place to pick the boys up from school. We shared a laugh and he was off. He talked to John for a quick minute and then he hopped in his truck. As he began to drive away, I stood in the front window and watched him until I couldn't see his tail lights anymore; not realizing that it would be my last time seeing my son alive.

I went on about my day, continued laundry as planned and was deciding on dinner for the evening. It was about 10:40 am when I received the first notification on social media with just my name under a photo of my son, then another under the same photo with my sons name, then the last one with a phone number... my heart began to race. I immediately knew something was wrong - my soul told me so. I picked up the phone and dialed through my tears as I ran for the front door. "Hello, what's going on?" A loud voice on the other end of the phone said "there was an accident, a bad accident, it was all my fault he's really hurt and not moving, help!" I'm in a complete panic, as I run to the door screaming "What happened to my baby?! Tell me now! What happened to my son? Where is he? Where are you? Where's the accident? What happened? Please tell me!" The phone went dead, then rang back almost immediately. The voice still loud and yelling " It's my fault! It's my fault!" Another voice got on the phone and called me by my last name. She was asking questions that I didn't care to answer. Ma'am where is my son?!? Is he going to be okay? She politely said, "No ma'am, but I need you to listen to me and get here safe." Get there safe? How could I? After what you just said to me? I don't remember how I continued to drive, but I made it to where her voice lead me. I parked my car and began to run towards the officer standing behind some tape. One of the officers stopped me and said "Ma'am, you can't go any further." I said who I was and then I noticed two officers dressed in street clothes heading my way...my heart sank into my stomach, I began to feel dizzy. Why today? Why him? Why now Lord? I was telling him fifteen minutes prior to that phone call that I would see him later. How could this be?

The first officer that approached asked me a series of questions. I tried to answer as fast as I could, but I just couldn't think. Then he stopped and looked at me and said Mrs. Smith is your son Sean Smith; I said "yes", he held my hand and said, "I'm sorry ma'am, but he didn't make it." I don't know if you all remember the test on the television networks with the loud beeps, but that's how I felt. I couldn't hear a thing. My entire world stopped at that moment. I had so many unanswered questions...how could he be gone? We just left each other 15 min ago. It's not him... yeah that's it, they made a mistake. He's on his way to work. I just need to find my cell phone and call him to clear all this up. I fell to the concrete and honestly don't remember anything else he may have said. I remember waking up and being tucked in a seat belt in the back of a patrol car and the medic approaching. I was given a bottled water and asked another series of questions...are you okay? You said you were having chest pain? You also stated that this was the worse pain you ever felt in your life? Medical help is here...would you like to be seen?

I was staring at them, but I couldn't really understand what was going on and how life was happening to me so fast while I was alone. Why? What did I do to deserve this? What did my child do to deserve this? Did he suffer? How did he die? I just wanted to hold my child and let him know I was there, but I could never get that opportunity, he was gone and all while being surrounded by complete strangers. He was mine and he was loved, how can this be? I'm supposed to protect them from all harm, and be there to make all things better. But this was completely out of my hands. My heart was aching and my soul needed my son so badly. I just wanted him to know I was there.

A deep voice from the right side of the vehicle asked, "Ma'am, is there anyone we can call for you?" I don't know. I tried my husband several times while enroute and my mother was working; my poor children were in school. I wanted to keep the information to myself, so my family wouldn't feel the pain that was cutting me down to my bones; but I was screaming for some help and a familiar face. I was taken to the police station, where they then began calling my family one by one. My mom's number was the only number besides my husbands I could remember at the time. They continued asking questions that I just couldn't answer; I couldn't even remember where my husband worked. I was in a desperate place with nowhere to go and all alone.

My mom arrived first, puzzled as to why she was there and why she was picked up by an officer. she knew something dreadful was going on by the look on my face. I fell into her arms and said "Ma, he was in an accident and he didn't make it! My son is gone and I can't even see him.".She began to yell, "Who didn't make it? Not my grandson! No! They have the wrong person. This can't be right. This can't be right." She went on and on, and I couldn't even understand the words she was saying. As we sat in silence, my middle child walked in, "Ma what's wrong why are we here?" "Son, there was an accident and your brother didn't make it." "What?! Man!!!" He sat at the table at the far end and began to stare into space, not saying a word. A few minutes passed and the baby walked in. "Mommy, what's wrong? What happened?" I began to just break down. Lord, I was tired and wanted help. Why was I put into this position to have to repeatedly say those words to the people I love the most. I had to tell this child, who looked up to his brother so much, that he would never see him alive again; that that day was the last time his brother would drop him at school. I could barely speak before my other son said loudly, "Sean died! He died!". My youngest child began sobbing uncontrollably, asking the same questions I did. He picked up Stanley's phone that was on the table and began dialing Sean's number...over and over and over again. He looked at me and said "Ma he won't answer me. He won't answer me". What was I to do? How could I stop them from hurting when I was completely shattered on the inside? I hugged them all and didn't say a word, while tears continued to pour from my eyes.

The Chaplin came in and offered some words and a prayer that I honestly didn't want to hear. This was not supposed to happen to my family. I thought we were doing everything right. I was angry. I mean. I know I had my kids out of wedlock, but they all belong to the same man that I've known since I was 12 years old. We got married and vowed to love one another until death do us part in a church in front of family and friends. We moved to the best neighborhoods, sent them to the best schools and even relocated to give the boys a better life, how dare God do this to me, to us, to him...why?!

"...until we meet again
Those special memories of you
Will always bring a smile
If only I could have you back
For just a little while
Then we could sit and talk again
Just like we used to do
You always meant so very much
And always will do too
The fact that you're no longer here
Will always cause us pain
But you're forever in our hearts
Until we meet again."

—MAYA ANGELOU

As we all continued to sob in silence, Stanley's phone began to ring; it was my husband. As my son answered, all he kept saying was "Dad Sean died...he died Dad". He handed me the phone and said, "Ma, Dad said there was a mistake. He's alive and at the hospital." For just a split second, I had a little bit of hope, but I was on the scene. I knew better. I knew what my husband was saying was not true. When my husband checked his phone, he had several missed calls from several different people. He had spoken to several of the boys' friends and they had received information from the other boy involved and gave my husband the wrong information. As I tried my best to get those words out of my mouth, again he broke down and yelled, "No no no, don't tell me this about my son! No no no!" I just threw the phone down, within 20 minutes, he arrived at the station. We all embraced one another and began what was going to be a very long journey of firsts.

After a twenty minute drive, we had all arrived home, but the drive really felt like three hours. None of us knew what to do or how to feel. Our world, as we knew it, had been completely flipped upside down. The house was cold, even though it was near 80 degrees outside, and uncomfortably quiet. I had to make phone calls to the ones nearest and dearest to me, but how in the hell do I pull myself together to do that? The very first call was made to my dad " Hello Daddy, Sean is gone." "What do you mean he's gone baby? Talk to me." As I sobbed uncontrollably, my Dad yelled, "What's going on?! Talk to me!" "He died today, Daddy. He was in a bad car accident..." The rest of the conversation is a complete blur, besides his last words as we said goodbye. I can remember my Dad saying "I'm coming baby. Daddy will be there soon." I hung up and decided who would be next. I called my nephew. who has always been more like my son. I wanted to hear his voice, and for him to hear it from me. "Hello, are you sitting down?" "Why? What's up Aunty?" "I have some bad news. There was an accident and Sean didn't make it." COMPLETE silence, then a loud noise in the background. "No Aunty! What happened? Not my brother! Not my brother! You're lying!" He was screaming and yelling and throwing things around his apartment. I couldn't talk anymore. I had just broken another one of our boys hearts. I couldn't even listen to him anymore. My husband took the phone and tried his best to calm him through the phone. I then called two friends; as close as I thought I was to these two people, I wanted them to know and hear it from me, and I needed to know that they would be there for me.

As I dialed the numbers through my tears, the phone rang and she answered, "Hello?" I was screaming her name and trying to tell her. She began to cry and said, "Please tell me what's wrong! You're scaring me!" I was finally able to get the words out, and they cut me deep. I couldn't believe I was saying those words over and over again to the ones we loved. She told me she loved me and we hung up. My next phone call was to another friend, one I'll never forget. The phone rang two times she answered, "Hello?" As I cried and tried to get those words out yet again, I could tell I was on the speaker in the car. "Can you pick up the phone?" I asked., "I'm driving. What's up?" "No, I need to tell you something. Please pick up." "I'm driving!" I just blurted out, "Sean died today in a car accident." She then picked up the phone and said she was sorry, but by that time, I just wanted off the phone with her. I had to call one more person; the person that I thought could give me the answers I needed. I searched for the number and hit send..."Hello, this is Sean's mom, can I please speak with John?" The voice was very calm and he said "He just walked in the house, but he's coming right back. Can you hold please?" "Yes, I can hold." It seemed like it took him forever to get to the phone. "Hello? Hey Mrs. Smith, What's up?" "Can you please tell me exactly what happened today? You stated that it was your fault. John, what happened to my son?" "I mean, we wrecked...we just wrecked," He went on and on and then started talking about things that had nothing to do with the accident...like the fact that he had just gotten paid that day and he was heading to cash his check. What I wanted to hear was the truth...you were playing in and out of traffic and caused my son to be hit by an 18 wheeler that was trying to avoid hitting you, but I would never hear those words. That was the worst conversation I had that day! I felt hopeless, like my life didn't matter - especially at my lowest point. I mean, I'm his mom begging for you to be honest, and even in that moment, everything was still about him, the person who had made it out alive with barely a scratch.

I was extremely angry. I couldn't talk to anyone else that day. I didn't want to, but the phones would not stop ringing.I couldn't even call the person closest to me. How could I? I knew once I heard her voice I would lose it. My sister loves my children as her own and I knew she would be just as devastated as we were. I put a terrible burden on my husband, because he continued to call and answer both his phone and mine. Family and friends were calling or texting just to say they love us and would be there for us. While others were making arrangements to come to our home. I wanted the world to stop!

The very next day, October 6, 2016 was the first day of the rest of our lives - forever changed. The morning started very different ,of course. I don't think any of us got more than two hours of sleep that night. I wanted it all to be a nightmare that I would awake from, but when I opened my eyes to the ringing of the doorbell at 5am, I knew my life had drastically changed forever.

Over the next 10 days, our lives were totally rearranged. From house guests, arrangements, travel information, programs, to family fights/arguments about what they thought may be best. I had been thrown into a world that I didn't ask to be in, and that I/we knew nothing about. We are forever grateful for those who would not leave our side and held our hands the entire way, but I just wanted my old life back; you know, the one I complained about from time to time; the one I thought was terrible at times. I found myself pleading with God…"If I could just have him back, I promise to never complain about anything ever again." I wanted to hug him hold him just one last time, but that opportunity was gone and would never return.

As my family said our final goodbyes to my son, my heart died, and was buried right next to him. I didn't want to be anything anymore, not a wife, a mother, a sister, NOTHING! I spent over one month in bed, without eating and without being anything good for anyone - not even myself. I contemplated suicide and knew exactly when I would act on it. I was at my lowest point, even though I thought I had already reached that state. I wanted to disappear; my soul was aching, and I wanted nothing to do with life. I felt as if no one knew the unbearable pain I was feeling - not even the people closest to me, who I'm sure felt the pain just as deep as I did.

In these terrible times, support was very important and mine was amazing. I wanted to just throw in the towel on life, but they wouldn't allow me to. My husband was a great support; he carried the weight of the world on his shoulders, not really taking the moment he needed to grieve himself. My sisters would not leave my side, be it a group text chat, group video chat or my closest sister taking time off to spend a month of her time in another state, away from her everyday life with my nephew. She just wanted to help with my children, support my husband, and push me to live again. I wanted to kick her out because she was driving me crazy with, "Get up. Let's walk. Let's go to the mall. Let's cook. How about we go out to eat tonight? Have you showered today? Let's take the kids out."... I just wanted her to let me be. She took on the role as my boys' mom, because at that time, I just couldn't be anything to anyone.

The time finally came for her and my nephew to go home; I was sad, but happy at the same time. I wanted to just lay in bed, without being bothered. I was still receiving phone calls from family, friends and coworkers, I didn't want to talk to anyone. Some people just wouldn't let up on me and were there to stay, but most people had gone back to their normal lives and forgot that we ever existed.

One of my coworkers continued to call, or have others call me, I couldn't figure her out; she kept saying in her messages that she had something for me. So, I thought,"Fine, send it by the one coworker/friend who I spoke with on a daily basis." She finally said, "It's not a gift, but a phone number of a mother who also suffered the loss of a child." I thought to myself, "Great, here we go. I will forever be labeled and put into a category that I never asked for." I took the number, but I was so bitter that I never thought I would use it.

I was left alone and everyone was finally out of the house. This was my time. Finally, I could act on the feelings I'd been having over the past few months. I picked up the phone and dialed the number that was given to me for the first time. I needed to hear from another mom. I wanted to know her story, but she was busy and couldn't talk at that moment. I acted on my emotions...I went to my son's room and lay in his bed crying, and again, asking why?!? I went into my closet, took the gun down, made sure it was loaded and took the safety off. I took a few deep breaths and pulled the trigger, but nothing happened. By this time my husband was beating on the doors because he had left his keys in the house. My phone was ringing and ringing, but I refused to look at it. I squeezed the trigger one last time before my husband came running up the stairs. He couldn't believe what I tried to do. He handed me the phone and it was my mother in law...I cried and told her exactly how I was feeling we talked for a few moments before she made me promise a few things before hanging up. I hugged my husband and told him I just couldn't go on the way I was. I knew at that very moment I needed help!

"Learn to get in touch with the silence within yourself, and know that everything in life has purpose. There are no mistakes, no coincidences, all events are blessings given to us to learn from."

—ELISABETH KUBLER- ROSS

I gathered my thoughts and showered. I was told to pray, but how could I? My world had just been ripped apart, and God did nothing to stop it! I was tired of hearing "Things will be better soon." How do you know this? "You'll be alright." Says who? I'm in pain! "God knows best." Oh does he? "He's in a better place." How in the world do you know that?! "Everything gets better with time." Says who? "God bless you and your family" blah blah blah. I didn't want to hear any of that shit any more. I couldn't help but think that if they were in my shoes, how would they feel? It's so easy to blurt out anything, when your walk is so different than mine.

After my shower, I sat in the dark and my phone rang; it was the woman I had called to talk with about my feelings, to learn her story, and most of all, to learn how in the hell she was still going. We began to talk and she shared her story with me. I just couldn't believe it; I mean, this woman was the strongest person I'd ever met. She was truthful in every way with me. She told me how selfish I was for even thinking that suicide was the answer. I needed to hear those words. She kept asking me why my other children didn't get to have me as they had before. Why weren't they as important as they had been before? They didn't ask for this to happen. I was selfish in thinking my pain meant more than theirs. She was right…they needed me and my poor husband was left to deal with it all, with no help from me. I cried alone. I isolated myself in any way that I could from the ones who were closest to me. I was so selfish in my pain, that I couldn't even see theirs.

Before we hung up, she promised to keep up with me. Once we were off the phone, I decided to look for professional help. I had sunk into a deep depression and was putting my own horrible feelings and emotions before the ones who needed me most. It was time for a change that only I had control over.

The single greatest thing you can do to change your life today would be to start being grateful for what you have right now!

-OPRAH WINFREY

I started looking for help anyway I could; I Googled therapists, asked coworkers, etc. After several attempts with others, I finally found someone with whom I felt comfortable. Finding someone who was compassionate and caring was very tough. I was blessed to have stumbled upon a good one. I had my first session over the phone. I can remember crying on a Sunday with nowhere to go and no one to turn to. I dialed her number and she answered. I was so shocked that I almost didn't know what to say…I began speaking through my tears and telling her the pain that I was going through and why. She listened and asked just the right amount of questions. She didn't pry, and allowed me time to rest and continue without rushing me through what I had to say. After we spoke for an hour or so, she encouraged me to start journaling and said that she wanted to meet with me. I scheduled my first session that day. I was so comfortable with her; I felt so much lighter - like a weight had been lifted directly off my shoulders.

I was trying to be more attentive at home. I tried to pay attention to the things I had missed over the past few months. I did things with the boys - even if it was just a walk around our development. I encouraged them to continue the sports they had been playing and I even started to journal as I had before. Writing and music has always been my therapy, but I couldn't do any of that anymore due to my pain. The pain I felt after losing my child was unbearable; my only focus was sleeping, so I wouldn't have to think about how I would continue with life. But I was ready to beat this. I wanted a new normal for my family. I wanted them to see me fight for better - not only for me, but most importantly, for them.

My first therapy session was approaching and the anxiety was killing me. I had no idea what this experience was going to be like, but I was ready to do anything to begin to feel better. I did exactly what she suggested and had been writing my thoughts and emotions down daily. As simple as that seems, it was a huge help. Just being able to get the thoughts out of my head and heart and onto a piece of paper was a relief. I was preparing myself like it was the first day of school. The day had come and I was ready. When I finally met her, it felt as if I had known her forever. She had this amazing glow about her. She smiled and embraced me. We walked together to her office and before we began the session, she made sure I was comfortable.

During that session, I talked about Sean and cried; I also laughed. I shared my journal entries and cried more, but I was on my way to finding my way back to me. Before I left the office, I scheduled my next visit; at that moment, I was determined to force change out of my situation. I continued to go to counseling on a weekly basis and was committed to journaling daily. I never realized how effective journaling was until I actually started revealing my entries. Releasing bottled up feelings definitely has some sort of healing power.

As the weeks went by, and as I continued to study myself and my emotions, I learned how and what to do in times that I needed my son most. Crying in the middle of the night, not sleeping, some days not wanting to get out of bed. I knew that those moments were normal and that I shouldn't punish myself for my feelings. I learned to have my moment and move past it with the knowledge that life will continue to happen, but we must learn how to balance the good and bad. I was blessed with a family that loved me unconditionally - on my good and bad days. We, as a family, were very blessed to have one another in those dark days. I refused to allow my depression to win. Suffering with mental illness can be a huge burden - especially if you're struggling alone. Having someone to depend on, whether its a close friend, family member, therapist, coworker, or spouse. Whomever it may be, we all need someone we can trust.

There's nothing worse than depending on someone to have your back and be by your side, and they turn their back or repeat your deepest darkest secrets. I can honestly say that I have been in a situation where I trusted someone and my deepest secrets were revealed. I had to learn to trust again, and that was not easy. But we have to learn to trust, because it may be the only tool that will help during difficult times. We need to do a self check weekly or daily if needed. Life causes all sort of feelings, and if we're not careful or fully aware, we could drown in our emotions before we even realize we have a problem.

Mental health disorders or mental illness refers to a large range of mental instability. Some of the signs that we are experiencing mental illness are irritability, anxiety, sadness, fear, constant worry, social withdrawal, poor sleeping habits, alcoholism and a dramatic change in diet.

Mental illness comes in many forms, but we are so afraid to speak on it; to say out loud that we suffer from some form of mental illness. We don't want to be judged or labeled by those looking at us, who in many cases, are suffering just as we are. Mental health issues are something that we can recover from, with the right steps taken to do so. It is not a death sentence and we have to start acknowledging when we need help.

Mental health is defined as a person's condition with regard to their psychological and emotional well being. We as people hate to discuss mental health because it's like some sort of disease we all want to avoid catching. Honestly, I think we all as humans suffer from some form of mental illness, whether its depression, anxiety, personality disorders, mood disorders, phobias, PTSD, and eating disorders - just to name a few. We refuse to even admit that we are struggling, because for some strange reason, "per society" it's a sign of weakness. So what do we do? We hide behind our smiles, careers, families, and our children; we refuse to admit to anyone, especially ourselves, that we NEED help.

How am I feeling? That's a simple enough question, right? But due to our ever so busy lives, we fail to even think of asking ourselves that question. Usually, upon waking in the morning, before you can even think to yourself, it's time to start the day. If you have children, the day can be a bit busier. We all have a deadline and some place to be. By the end of the day, who has time to think before showering the stress of the day away and crawling into bed before its time to start all over again? We must make a conscious effort to save ourselves. No one is going to do that for us!

Love yourself so that love will not be a stranger when it comes. -Jenifer Lewis

As you become more clear about who you really are, you'll be able to decide what is best for you the first time around.

—OPRAH WINFREY

Journal

Where there is no struggle, there is no strength.

-OPRAH WINFREY

This weeks goals

- ♡ ....
- ♡ ....
- ♡ ....

How I plan to reach these goals

- ♡ ....
- ♡ ....
- ♡ ....

Appointments

1. ....
2. ....
3. ....

New habits

- ♡ ....
- ♡ ....
- ♡ ....
- ♡ ....

MEDITATION TIPS

1. Find a nice quiet space
2. Make it comfortable
3. Start some calming music
4. Focus
5. Sit and enjoy the calm

Meditation doesn't have to be an everyday thing but learning to break away for just a few minutes a day or week can help with stress and balance. Start with five minutes...

This week's focus:
....

Sunday | Monday

Tuesday | Wednesday

Thursday	Friday

Saturday	Notes

My personal thoughts

This weeks goals

♡ ....
♡ ....
♡ ....

How I plan to reach these goals

♡ ....
♡ ....
♡ ....

Appointments

1. ....
2. ....
3. ....

New habits

♡ ....
♡ ....
♡ ....
♡ ....

Meditation Music used ♪ ....

How many minutes ⏰ ....

It was hard this week because ....
....
....
....
....

This week's focus:

Sunday

Monday

Tuesday

Wednesday

Thursday	Friday
Saturday	Notes

You have within you right now everything you need to deal with whatever the world can throw at you.

-UNKNOWN

My personal thoughts

This weeks goals

♡ ....
♡ ....
♡ ....

How I plan to reach these goals

♡ ....
♡ ....
♡ ....

Appointments

1. ....
2. ....
3. ....

New habits

♡ ....
♡ ....
♡ ....
♡ ....

Meditation Music used ♪ ....

How many minutes ⏰ ....

It was hard this week because ....
....
....
....
....

This week's focus:

Sunday

Monday

Tuesday

Wednesday

Thursday

Friday

Saturday

Notes

That which does not kill us makes us stronger.

This weeks goals

♡ ....
♡ ....
♡ ....

How I plan to reach these goals

♡ ....
♡ ....
♡ ....

Appointments

1. ....
2. ....
3. ....

New habits

♡ ....
♡ ....
♡ ....
♡ ....

Meditation Music used ♪ ....

How many minutes ⏲ ....

It was hard this week because ....
....
....
....
....

This week's focus:
....

Sunday | Monday

Tuesday | Wednesday

Thursday

Friday

Saturday

Notes

My personal thoughts

This weeks goals

♡ ....
♡ ....
♡ ....

How I plan to reach these goals

♡ ....
♡ ....
♡ ....

Appointments

1. ....
2. ....
3. ....

New habits

♡ ....
♡ ....
♡ ....
♡ ....

Meditation Music used ♪ ....

How many minutes ⏱ ....

It was hard this week because ....
....
....
....
....

This week's focus:
....

| Sunday | Monday |

Tuesday | Wednesday

Thursday

Friday

Saturday

Notes

There are only two options make progress or make excuses.

My personal thoughts

This weeks goals

♡ ....
♡ ....
♡ ....

How I plan to reach these goals

♡ ....
♡ ....
♡ ....

Appointments

1. ....
2. ....
3. ....

New habits

♡ ....
♡ ....
♡ ....
♡ ....

Meditation Music used 🎵 ....

How many minutes 🕐 ....

It was hard this week because ....
....
....
....
....

This week's focus:
....

Sunday	Monday
Tuesday	Wednesday

Thursday

Friday

Saturday

Notes

Stay patient and trust your journey.

My personal thoughts

This weeks goals

♡ ....
♡ ....
♡ ....

How I plan to reach these goals

♡ ....
♡ ....
♡ ....

Appointments

1. ....
2. ....
3. ....

New habits

♡ ....
♡ ....
♡ ....
♡ ....

Meditation Music used ♪ ....

How many minutes ⏲ ....

It was hard this week because ....
....
....
....
....

This week's focus:
....

Sunday | Monday

Tuesday | Wednesday

Thursday

Friday

Saturday

Notes

My personal thoughts

This weeks goals

♡ ....
♡ ....
♡ ....

How I plan to reach these goals

♡ ....
♡ ....
♡ ....

Appointments

1. ....
2. ....
3. ....

New habits

♡ ....
♡ ....
♡ ....
♡ ....

Meditation Music used ♪ ....

How many minutes ⏲ ....

It was hard this week because ....
....
....
....
....

This week's focus:
....

Sunday	Monday

Tuesday	Wednesday

Thursday	Friday
Saturday	Notes

It's okay to not have it figured out.

My personal thoughts

This weeks goals

♡ ....
♡ ....
♡ ....

How I plan to reach these goals

♡ ....
♡ ....
♡ ....

Appointments

1. ....
2. ....
3. ....

New habits

♡ ....
♡ ....
♡ ....
♡ ....

Meditation Music used ♪ ....

How many minutes ⏱ ....

It was hard this week because ....
....
....
....
....

This week's focus:
....

Sunday | Monday

Tuesday | Wednesday

Thursday	Friday
Saturday	Notes

My personal thoughts

This weeks goals

♡ ....
♡ ....
♡ ....

How I plan to reach these goals

♡ ....
♡ ....
♡ ....

Appointments

1. ....
2. ....
3. ....

New habits

♡ ....
♡ ....
♡ ....
♡ ....

Meditation Music used 🎵 ....

How many minutes ⏰ ....

It was hard this week because ....
....
....
....
....

This week's focus:
....

Sunday	Monday
Tuesday	Wednesday

Thursday

Friday

Saturday

Notes

Be grateful for right now.

My personal thoughts

This weeks goals

♡ ....
♡ ....
♡ ....

How I plan to reach these goals

♡ ....
♡ ....
♡ ....

Appointments

1. ....
2. ....
3. ....

New habits

♡ ....
♡ ....
♡ ....
♡ ....

Meditation Music used ♪ ....

How many minutes ⏲ ....

It was hard this week because ....
....
....
....
....

This week's focus:

Sunday

Monday

Tuesday

Wednesday

Thursday

Friday

Saturday

Notes

Small steps everyday.

My personal thoughts

This weeks goals

♡ ....
♡ ....
♡ ....

How I plan to reach these goals

♡ ....
♡ ....
♡ ....

Appointments

1. ....
2. ....
3. ....

New habits

♡ ....
♡ ....
♡ ....
♡ ....

Meditation Music used ♪ ....

How many minutes 🕒 ....

It was hard this week because ....
....
....
....
....

This week's focus:
....

Sunday | Monday

Tuesday | Wednesday

| Thursday | Friday |

| Saturday | Notes |

A little progress each day adds up to big results.

www.ingramcontent.com/pod-product-compliance
Lightning Source LLC
Chambersburg PA
CBHW062027290426
44108CB00025B/2817